A Day in the Country

by Willis Barnstone

Pictures by Howard Knotts

Harper & Row, Publishers

NEW YORK   EVANSTON   SAN FRANCISCO   LONDON

A DAY IN THE COUNTRY

Text copyright © 1971 by Willis Barnstone
Pictures copyright © 1971 by Howard Knotts
All rights reserved. No part of this book may be used or reproduced in any manner whatsoever without written permission except in the case of brief quotations embodied in critical articles and reviews. Printed in the United States of America. For information address Harper & Row, Publishers, Inc., 49 East 33rd Street, New York, N.Y. 10016. Published simultaneously in Canada by Fitzhenry & Whiteside Limited, Toronto.

Library of Congress Catalog Card Number: 75-135771
Standard Book Number 06-020408-7 (Trade)
Standard Book Number 06-020409-5 (Harpercrest)

to:

Aliki

&

Robert Vassilios

&

Anthony Dimitrios

          WB

to:

Ilse, my wife

          HK

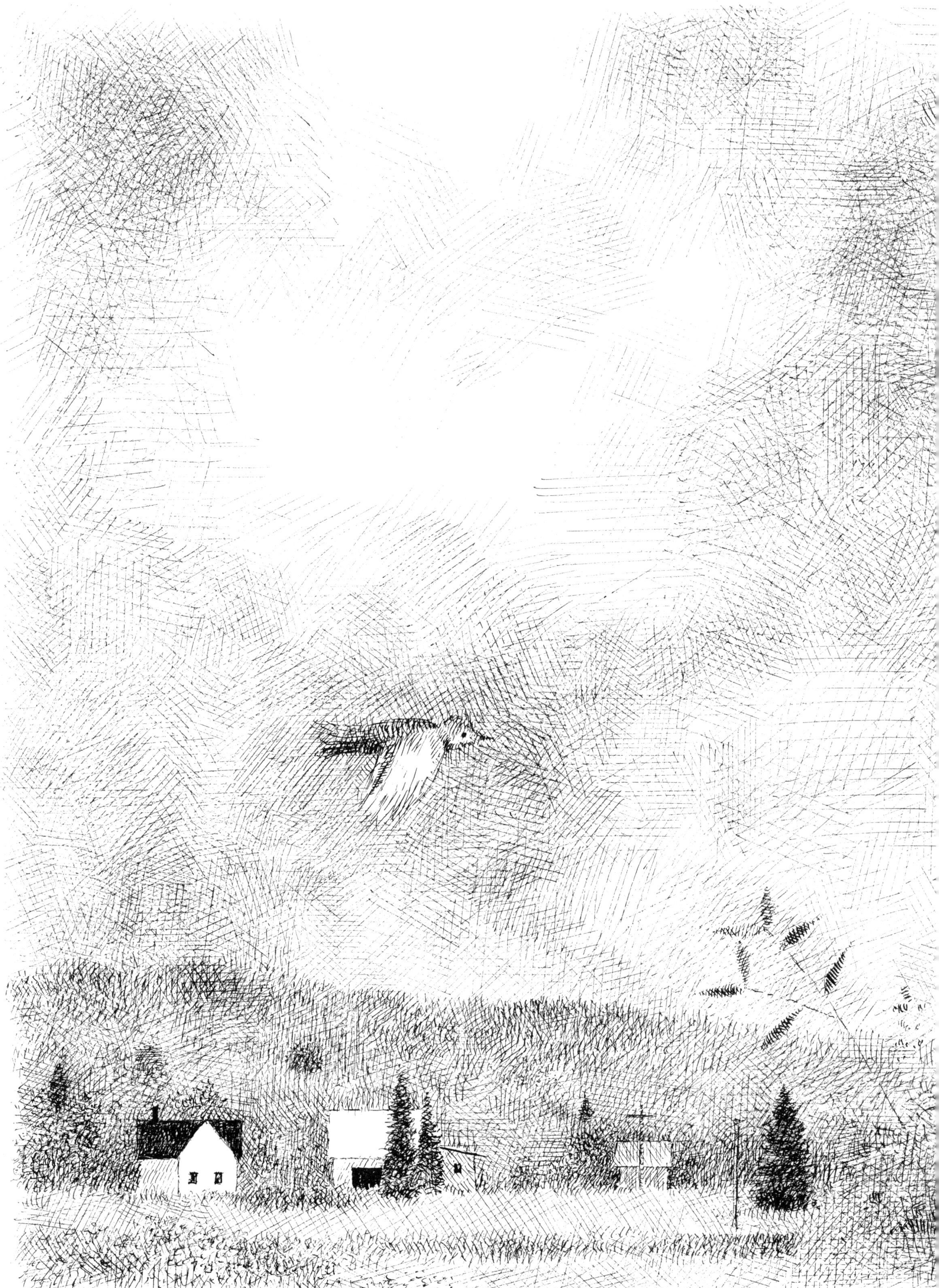

sky
sky
sky

early morning

a moon still up

three thin stars

and a mountain

the yellow

meadow lay

in cold sun.

some birds woke

and sang loud

to the worms

I woke in
a blue pool

crickets talked

on the phone

of the wind

to blue bugs

and woke up

the gold earth

and closed the

stars of sleep

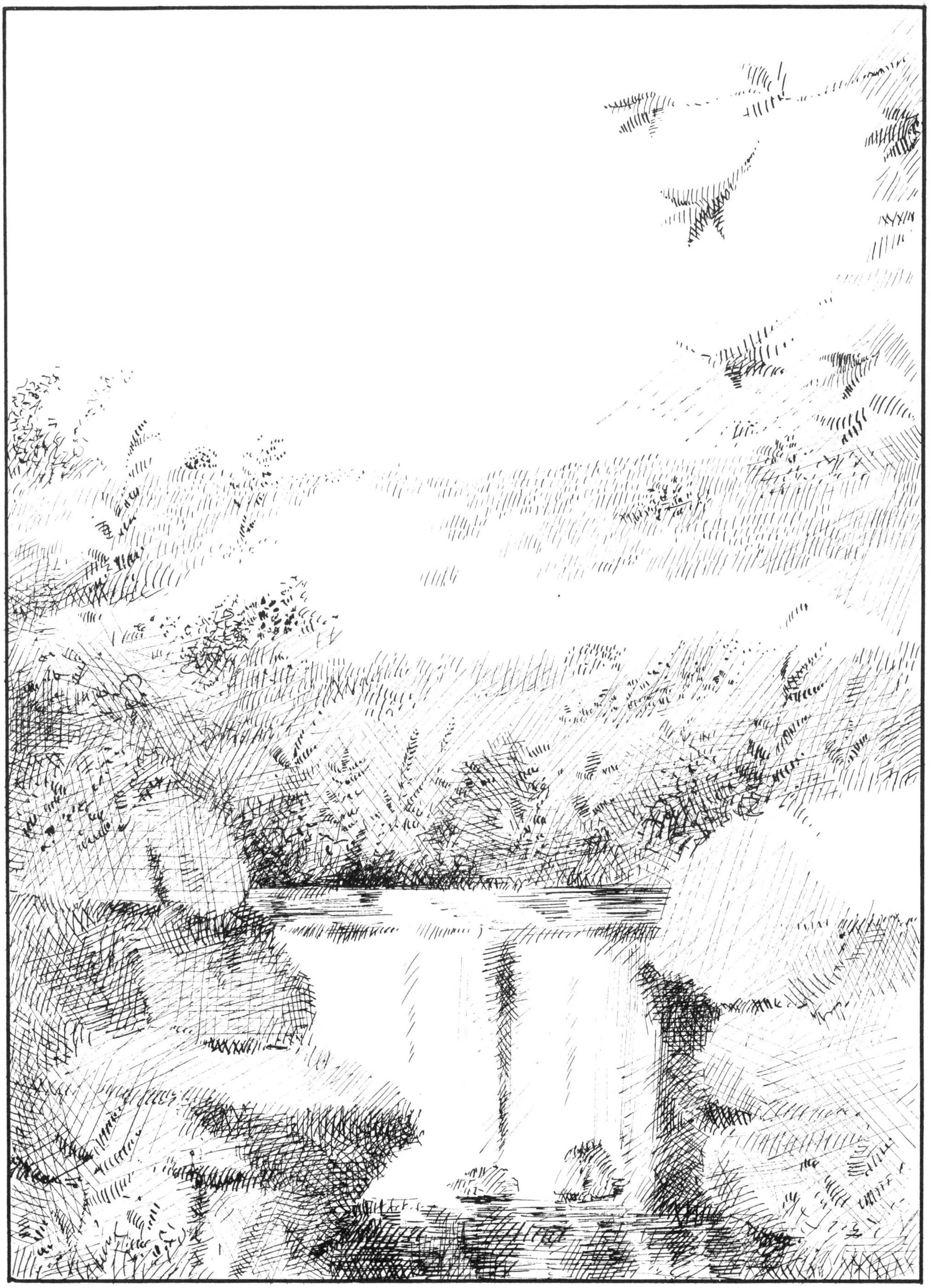

we put on sparkling
polo shirts and ran
outside.
    the wind
tasted like an apple

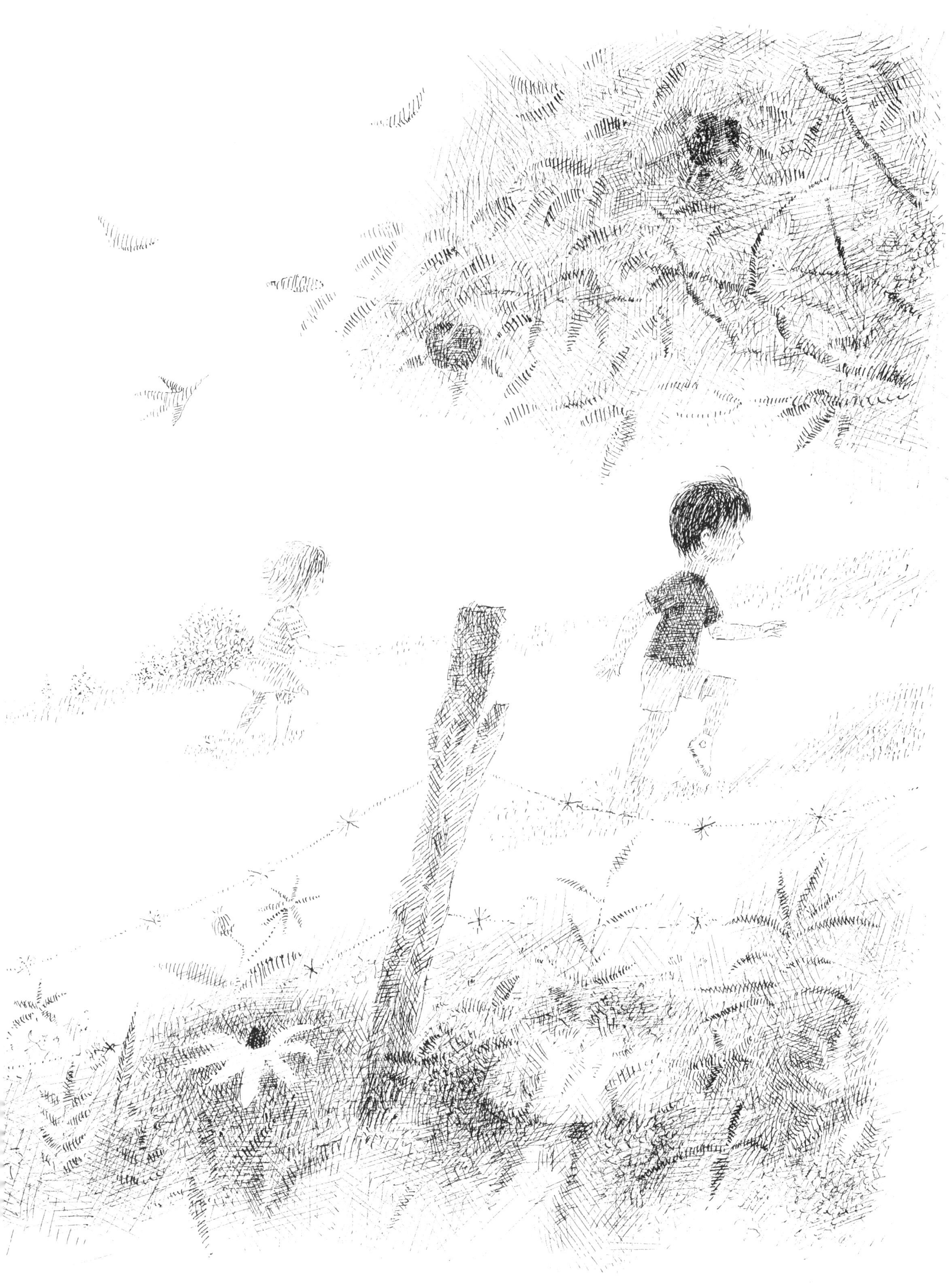

the sun was a yellow ship
on a sea of black-eyed Susans.
we went to the secret meadow

we all laughed
at breakfast.
I slopped milk
on my sneakers.
the girls laid
some clean plates
on rumpled grass

earlier the birds

sang. now we cheered

because the ball

came down from where

it was stuck in a

wild cherry tree

a girl called

to a big dumb

piece of air

and saw a flag

floating down

to a brook

o　o
　n　n
　n　n
o　o

I looked up
at blue air

the sun fell
through my eyes
to my heart

Z was our path
to reach the hill top

I tripped on a rock
and got a mouth-

ful of dirt and
lay like a beanbag

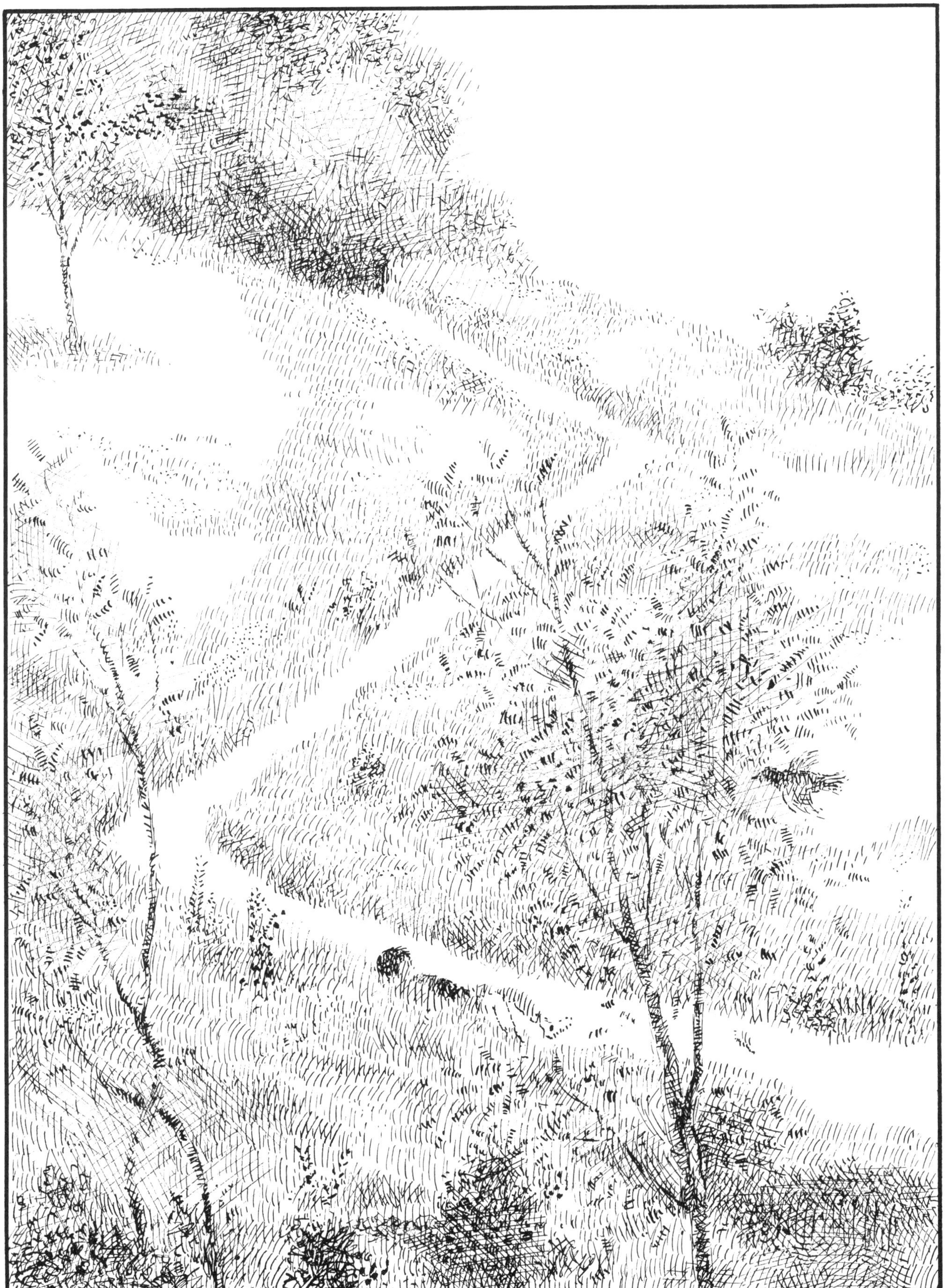

by evening the yellow
meadow was a big sack
of red eggs. our supper

was good old hot dogs
and a can of peas. we
dried off with Queen Anne's

lace and played baseball
till dark. I got a good
burn and felt the pins

of the enormous moon

```
o   o
m     n
m     n
o   o
```

again the yellow
meadow. I was not
happy before like
now!
    under the moon
my body was the color
of apple trees where
night air was hanging

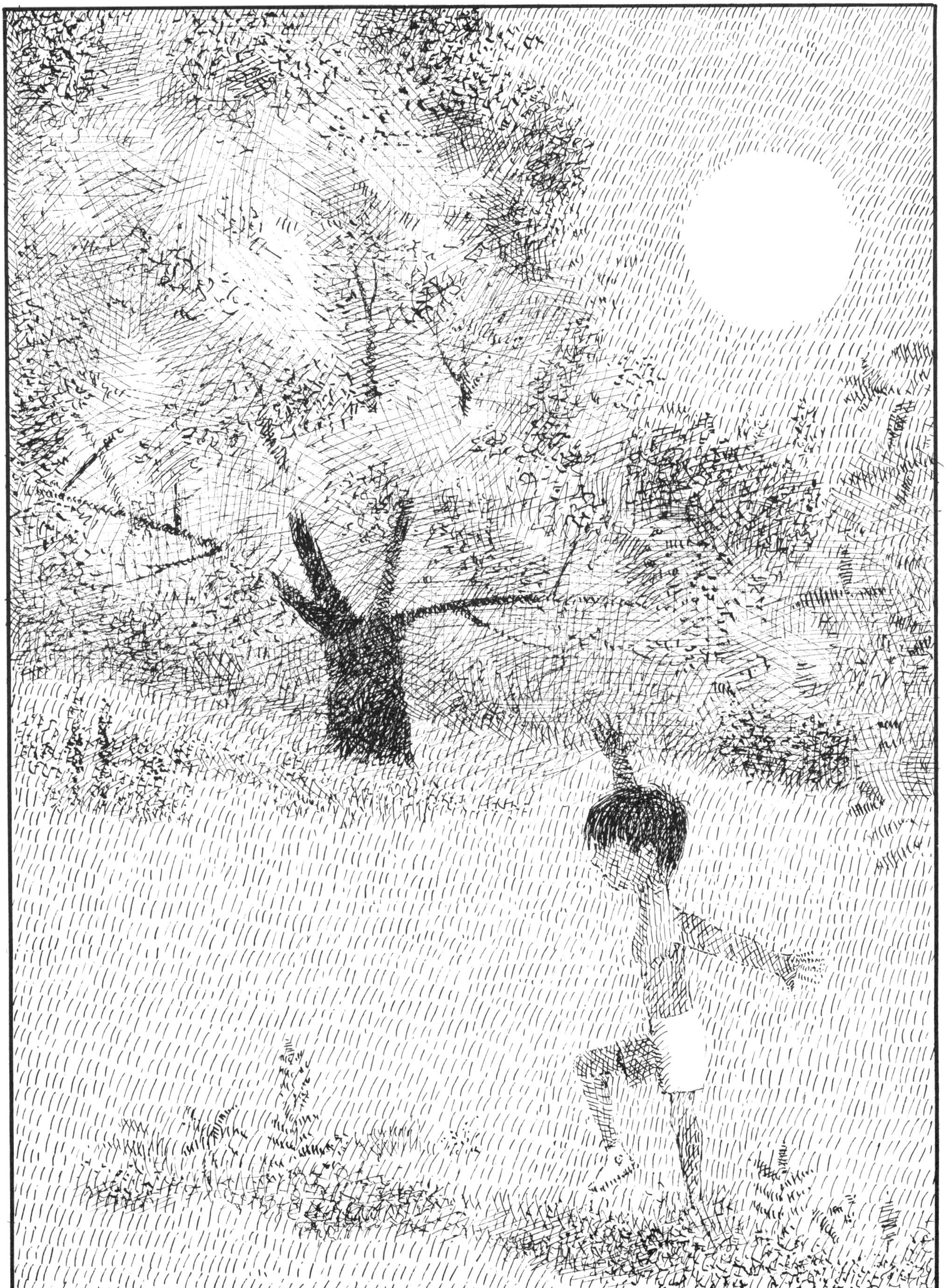

in the black airy

night I saw the

sky scratched with

a million crayons.

the forest was cold

hills without paint

s t a r s

s t a r s

s t a r s

I lay in bed

and the freezer

snored. tenor pipes

sang out in choir.

the water pump

was throbbing up

under my sleep

even in dream

the meadow was

a stork dozing

on a sunny tower.

the fields took care

of us. I wait

for morning light

and orange juice

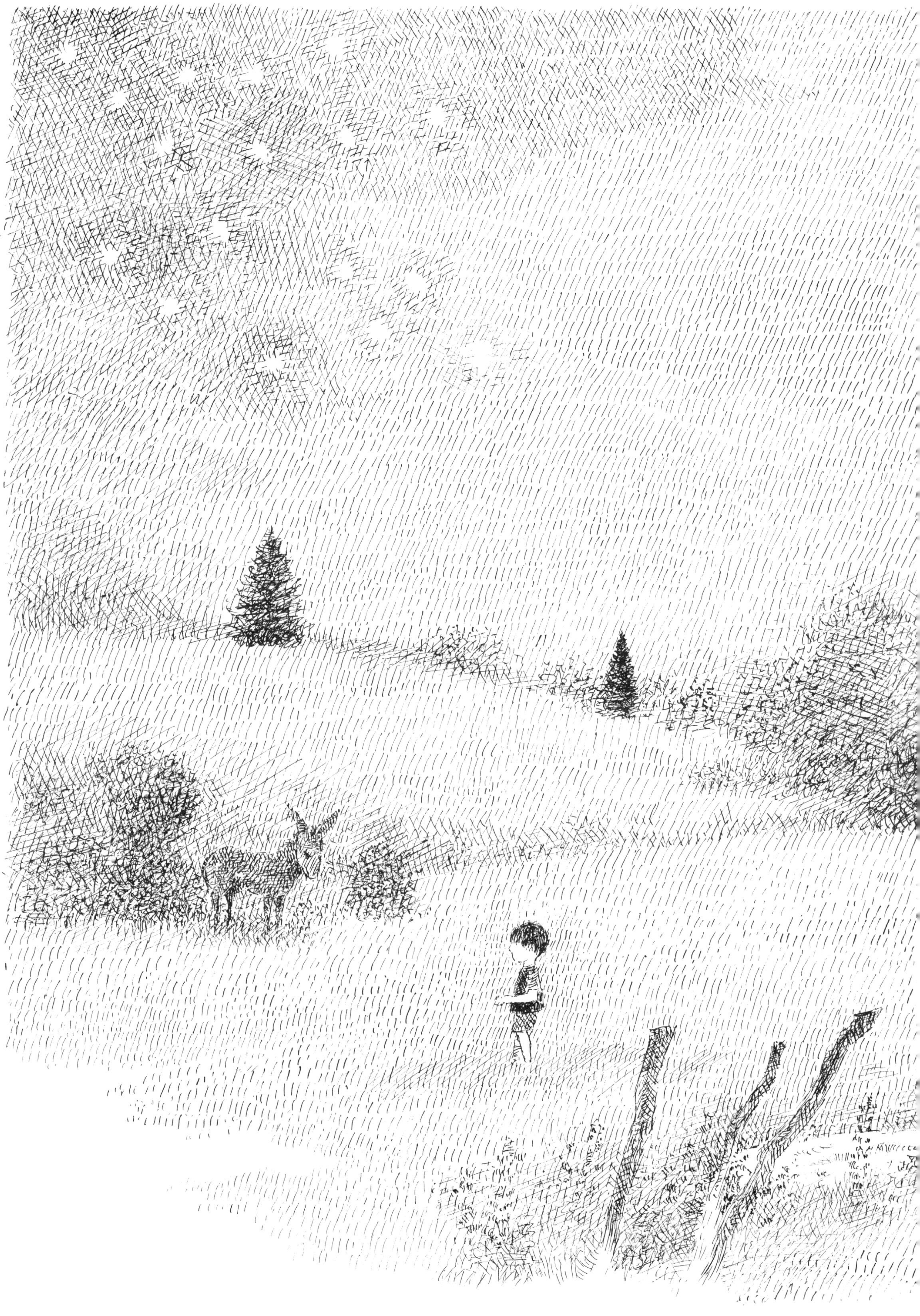

alone I leave
the house and
walk at dawn.

the cold dawn
fills me warm
with its rays

```
            sun

                     sun

         sun

                          sun


   sun             sun              sun
```

two birds

are sailing

in the

morning sun

high over

the secret meadow

how day
is good

how day
is good

how day
is good

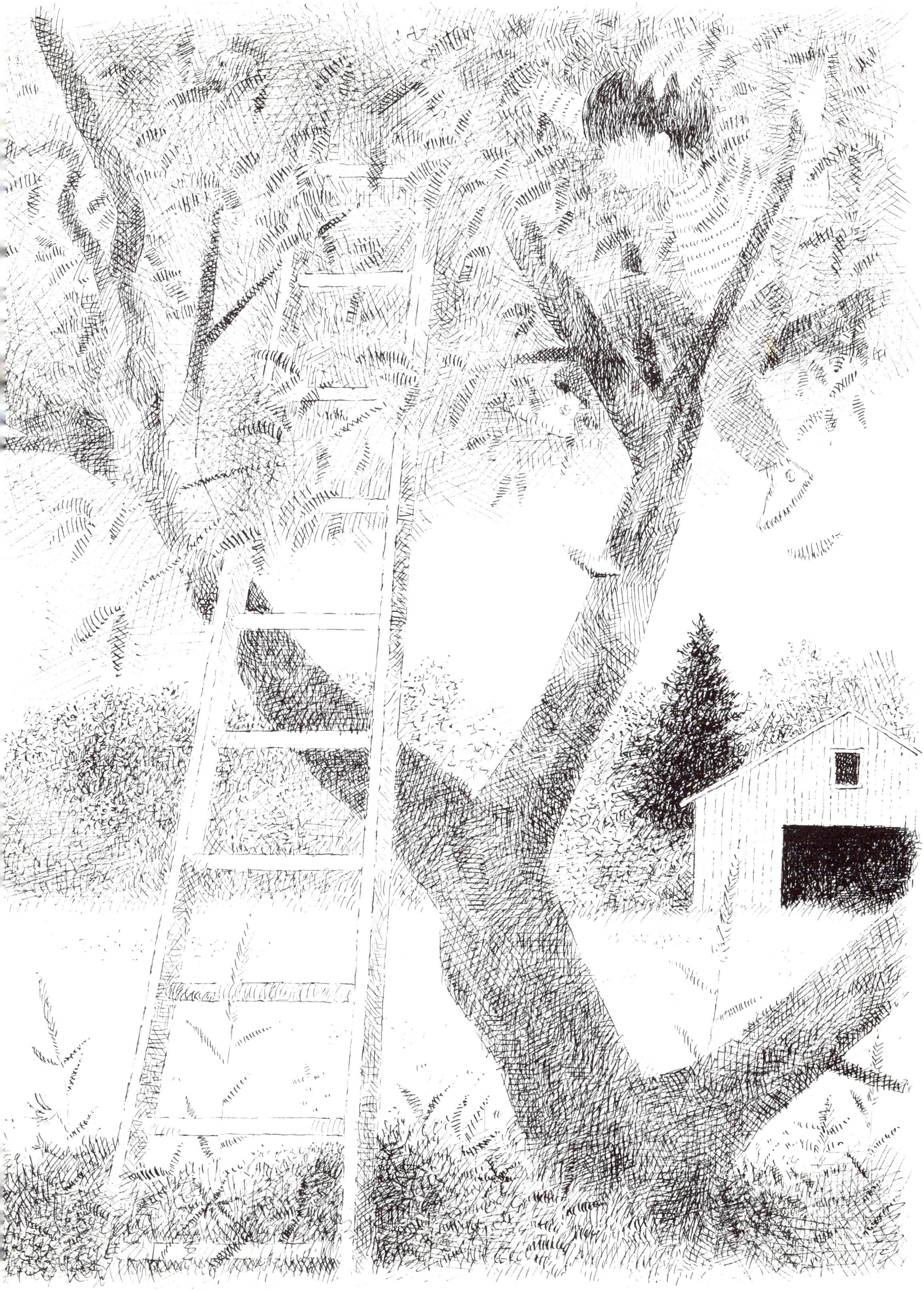

sky
sky
sky

DATE DUE

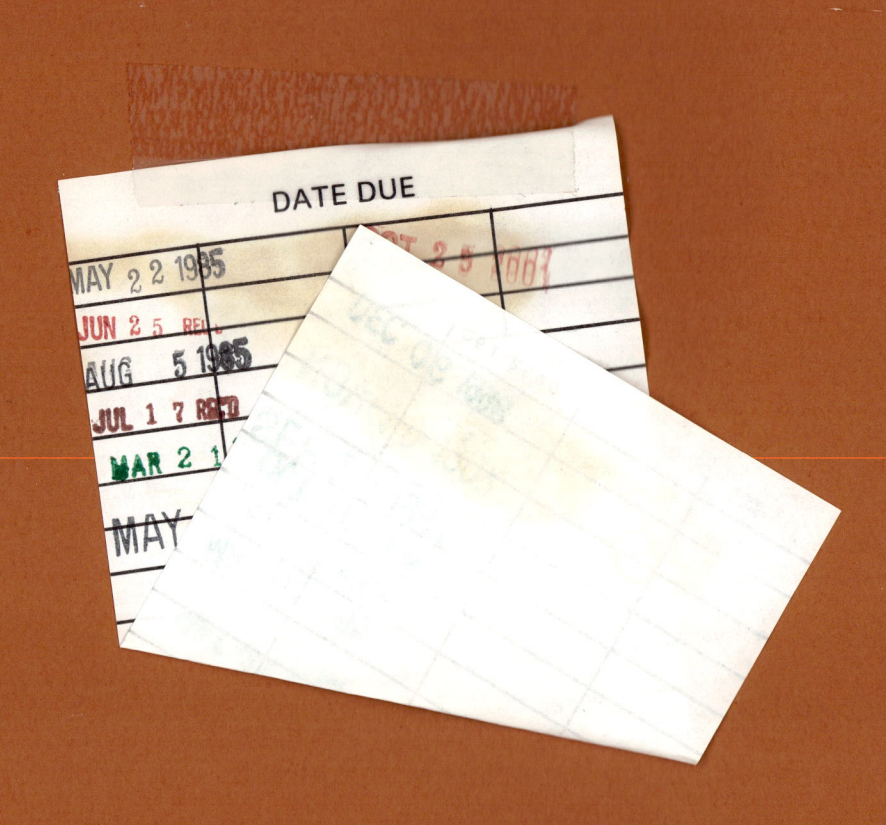

MAY 2 2 1985
JUN 2 5 REC'D
AUG 5 1985
JUL 1 7 REC'D
MAR 2 1
MAY